Town of Markham Public Libraries
Unionville Branch
15 Library Lane

Teenage Inforn

Personal Rel

MW01366635

	DATE DUE		
JUN 23, 1989			
MAY 1 4 1991			
FEB 1 0 1992			
MAR 20 1992			

Other titles in this series
So You Want to Try Drugs?
All about Drinking
Smoking—What's in it for You?
When Parents Split Up
How to Handle Your Parents
So You're Adopted!
When People Die
Who Do You Think You Are?
What about the Law?
The Healthy Body Book
Leaving Home

Personal Relationships
Dr Judy Greenwood is a Consultant in Community Psychiatry in Edinburgh, and is the author of COPING WITH SEXUAL RELATIONSHIPS.

Teenage Information Series

Personal Relationships

Judy Greenwood

Chambers

© Judy Greenwood 1986

All rights reserved. No part of this publication may be reproduced or transmitted in any form or by any means, electronic or mechanical, including photocopying, recording or any information storage or retrieval system without prior permission, in writing, from the publisher.

Published by W & R Chambers Ltd Edinburgh 1986

British Library Cataloguing in Publication Data

Greenwood, Judy
    Personal relationships. — (Teenage Information Series)
    1. Interpersonal relations
    I. Title II. Series
    302'.024055   HM132

ISBN 0 550 20566 7
ISBN 0 550 75219 6 student ed.

Illustrations by Hazel McGlashan

Contents

1. INTRODUCTION 1

2. COMMUNITY RELATIONSHIPS 3

3. WORKING RELATIONSHIPS 8

4. FRIENDLY RELATIONSHIPS 13

5. FAMILY RELATIONSHIPS 23

6. YOUR RELATIONSHIP WITH YOURSELF 37

7. SEXUAL RELATIONSHIPS 47

1. Introduction

Although this is only a small book, it is about the most important subject in the world—YOU. Every person is unique, which means that there is nobody else quite like you anywhere in the world. That statement applies even if you are an identical twin.

To begin with, you are officially registered and identified by your first name, your family name, your date of birth and the town and country in which you were born. But who you are is far more complex than that.

What sort of person are you?

Look at the picture of the hand opposite and think how it relates to you. Who you are—your identity— is not a simple thing at all, but varies constantly according to circumstances and to your relationship with the people around you.

Your country and the local community in which you live influence you — these can be called your community relationships.

Then there are your working relationships (the type of work you do, your relationship with the people at work), your personal friendships and your family relationships.

There is also your relationship with your inner self. Everyone has a personality that is their very own. Some of it you inherit from your mother and father, but a lot of it is not inherited. Instead, it develops over the years from the good and bad experiences of your life. It is this personality that controls your behaviour, your judgements and your temperament. It controls the person you choose to be.

Finally, there are your sexual relationships. Your gender (male or female) often influences the kind of things people say about you—'He's a typical boy', 'She's so unfeminine'. But your sexuality will also have important effects on all your adult relationships, particularly if you have a special boyfriend or girlfriend. Eventually you may marry and go on to have children of your own.

Look at the picture of the hand again and then read on. The remaining chapters in the book look at some of the aspects of each of these important relationships in your life. By the time you get to the end of it you should understand yourself and your personal relationships better.

2. Community Relationships

Your relationship with the outside world undoubtedly affects your identity. This governs how you are classified or labelled (delinquent, pedestrian, cyclist, witness). Have you ever travelled on a cross-channel ferry?

If you have, you will know that you board ship in Dover labelled a British citizen, and you disembark at Calais as a foreigner or alien. Which label suits you better?

Many young people nowadays, between jobs or after leaving school, take advantage of cheap travel abroad, staying in youth hostels or cheap student accommodation. What do you think are the benefits of being away from your own culture? Are there any long-term disadvantages to being a rolling stone?

Although you can choose whether you call yourself a foreigner or a native (once you have left school at least), there is one relationship you cannot avoid.

Your relationship with the planet Earth

We all rely on the planet Earth and its natural resources for our survival. In the past we have taken it for granted, but nowadays people recognise how much we should value this relationship with our planet. All sorts of world conservation organisations have evolved as we become more conscious that we are gradually eroding away our precious assets. The Earth is your responsibility as much as anyone else's.

Your relationship with your country

Once you reach the age of 18, you will be officially recognised as an adult, and, if you have grown up in this country, as a British national. We tend to take our nationality for granted—but stop and think what the label 'British citizen' implies for you.

Just as we have certain assumptions about the characteristics of Germans and Italians and Indians, so they have certain assumptions about the British *you*.

As well as being brought up in a British home, you

probably speak the English language, listen to British radio, and watch British television. You will have gone to a British school, learnt British history and geography, and be familiar with British songs and books. You will also have been subjected to British advertising and all your shopping will be done in British shops. You may attend one of the many churches in Britain. In other words, you are a product of the British way of life and the British culture.

Like everyone else, you will have the benefit of the British National Health Service and social security system, and all that the British government provides the country with, for example, transport, housing, police, defence, etc. Even if you go abroad, there will be a British consul to look after your interests if you get into difficulties. In fact, we take much of being British for granted, which is perhaps why it is good to escape from our country from time to time and discover the benefits or disadvantages of life in other countries. Do you approve of our laws on alcohol, and our laws for controlling traffic? Do you approve of British police, of cinema censorship, of the laws on indecency? Do you agree that there are certain things that should be illegal below the age of 16?

What do you give to your relationship with your country?

Probably a lot more than you think!

Although the British label influences you, you undoubtedly influence it. You (once you are 18) choose which political party will control the nation. You choose which radio and television programmes you want to listen to or watch. You choose which adverts you will follow up, which shops you will favour, and which clothes will be fashionable.

You will perhaps have less choice about paying taxes

and national insurance stamps; most things have VAT on them, and once you have a job you will pay income tax, and once you have a house you will pay rates. So you are contributing to the nation's wealth. You also contribute to the nation's defence system in times of war and to the general prosperity of the nation (or lack of it) in times of peace.

Never underestimate the power of public opinion and public pressure groups. There are many powerful influences on the British nation, such as the church, the government, the commercial world and the EEC, but public opinion has influence too, and that means YOU.

Your local community

The area close to your home, whether it is a town or a village, probably affects your identity as much as your country of origin does. Has it affected your accent? Once you have become adult, you can choose whether to continue living in your home town, or whether to move.

Look at the local amenities in your area. Are there any libraries, swimming pools, parks, local radio stations, discos, cycle tracks, cinemas, restaurants, sports facilities, local churches, youth clubs, women's groups, community centres and health centres?

Local amenities are partly provided by local government, the members of which are elected by you and your parents, or they may be financed by local commercial concerns. How important are these amenities for you? Will they become more important once you leave school? Do you have any role in any of them? People vary enormously in their level of commitment to their community. Only you can decide whether to become a local activist, a user of local resources, a complainer about what is missing, or a non-joiner! You make a club, an organisation or a disco successful by your attendance at it.

What else can you give in your relationship with your local community, apart from your support of its local resources? Well, it is you who decide whether the streets are to be covered with litter, whether walls are covered with graffiti, and windows broken, whether your dog messes the pavement, whether your local park is strewn with old bicycles and broken trees. Similarly, you decide on the level of noise on public transport or in the street at night, and whether the elderly and the handicapped in your area are well catered for, both in terms of public amenities and the occasional social visit by friendly neighbours like yourself. In fact, a local community, taken as a whole, is much greater than the sum of its individual amenities. It is largely the product of the people that live in it, and you are as important an inhabitant as anyone else in that respect. Your relationship with your community matters.

3. Working Relationships

What are you?

When asked that question, most people answer with their job description—'I'm a mechanic, a nurse, a hairdresser, a student'. Work roles are the most

commonly used identity labels, but it is important, in this time of unemployment, to remember that your work identity is only one aspect of the person you are.

Some people who have a job make their entire life centre on their work—they are labelled 'work-aholic'. They are like tall thin skyscrapers with few foundations and nothing to fall back on if their work role should fail. A sensible person's foundations and base would be centred on relationships: close personal relationships, friendships, and social relationships within the community; they would enjoy hobbies and sports as well as taking an interest in their work role. They would be shaped like a pyramid instead of a skyscraper and would be a lot more secure, both in and out of work.

Work labels can be both a help and a hindrance. They lead to false, sweeping generalisations about typical teachers, typical doctors, typical students and typical pupils.

Nevertheless, a job description does provide a useful pair of crutches to help you walk through life more securely. It helps other people to classify you and that makes them feel more comfortable with you. And it contributes to your personal identity. A work role often has a set of rituals, a set of clothes, and even a way of life attached to it. It is not simply a label.

School

You will be surprised to learn that school is a good rehearsal for your future working role, and that the institution of school has a lot in common with many of the institutions you will end up working in. For example, it gives you a job description that the community recognises, a regular timetable, rules and a chance to develop and get on. School means many things. Remember how important you felt in the last year of your primary school, and the contrast when you started at the big secondary school, suddenly overwhelmed by these gigantic fifth- and sixth-formers. How our perceptions of the school prefects change over the years! Our perceptions of the teachers change too.

Many people look back on their schooldays as the happiest days of their life, although few would have admitted they were very happy at the time. School is an important bridge between infancy and adult life.

Adult working roles

At the moment you may be agonising over your future work identity; your life will be affected by the decisions you make—whether to work indoors or outdoors, in the town or in the countryside, whether to aim for academic or manual work, whether to 'service' other people or to service machines, whether to do part-time, full-time, daytime or nightshift work.

Your work role picks up again the theme of school—it gives you something to do, a timetable, a description recognised by other people, a position in society.

Part-time work

Many people, particularly women with young children, find that the gains from a work role are such that they want to keep it in their lives in addition to their other roles, e.g. housewife, mother and wife. They may also have their own parents to care for, but an outside work role gives that extra financial independence, that feeling of having a place in society and a chance to meet people outside the home. Some men are also discovering that, with part-time work, they too can have more time for their home, their wife and their children. The difference between the sexes may in time become less noticeable. What do you think about this?

Unemployed people and 'I'm only a housewife'

Sometimes, people who have no employment other than looking after the home or themselves, struggle with their self-image and identity. Just as some people see work as the all-important thing in their lives, other people see not having a job as a total disaster. Yet some of you will face periods of unemployment because work is difficult to find. Others may choose not to work when their families are small. If you developed as a pyramid, with a wide base of interests and labels to your name, your identity will be able to cope without the work label. You will still be a citizen, you will still have all your close relationships, you will still have all your interests and hobbies, and, with luck, will be an active user of your local resources and a participant in many of your local community events. Fortunately for most people, the state welfare benefit system will ensure that you are adequately housed, clothed and fed, but it will be up to you yourself to ensure that your personal view of yourself, i.e. your identity, is also nurtured and fed.

The saying, all work and no play makes Jack a dull boy, is true the other way round too—all play and no work makes Jack a dull boy, unless he can find constructive ways of filling his time that make him feel good about himself and give him a sense of achievement, even without a pay packet at the end of the week.

4. Friendly Relationships

Most people need friends.

If you move to a new town or a new school, you rarely feel settled and relaxed until you have made at least one friend. Only then do you feel at home in your new environment.

It is difficult not to make friends at school, because you are thrown together daily with a large group of people more or less your own age. This is fortunate, because having friends makes growing up very much easier.

Why are friends important?

You start life completely dependent on your family, like a baby bird in a nest. Your whole environment is controlled and governed by your parents. This includes the food you eat, the clothes you wear, the toys you play with, the outings you have (or do not have). And your parents also influence your attitudes, values and beliefs about what is right and wrong and what to expect from the world. But by the time you reach the age of five or six, it gradually dawns on you that there is another world out there, full of other people like yourself, but with different attitudes, values and beliefs from those of your parents. To begin with, these people are likely to be your teachers and people on television programmes and perhaps some relatives, but quite soon you become significantly influenced by your friends.

By the time you have reached eight or nine, you are likely to be as concerned about keeping up with your friends as you are about pleasing your parents. Think back to when you were at primary school and think what you gained from those young friendships:
—someone to play with
—someone that could share secrets with you
—someone who was at the same stage of growing up as you.

You can probably think of many more.

Peer group pressures

Young friendships are important because they provide you with a stepping-stone, so that you can distance yourself from your parents' influence, and begin to challenge them from the safety of your gang or group. But, like most young people, you may have found that this stepping-stone of friendship is a slippery one. While trying to escape from the feeling of being too much under your parents' influence, you may have slipped into being too heavily influenced by friends and acquaintances of your own age (these are called your *peer group*). Just think back to when you were a little younger. Did you ever want a new bike, or clothes, or a record player just like your friends had?

Trying to follow the rest of the herd often helps you through a difficult patch when you are not sure who you are, what you want, or what you believe in. Gradually, though, you begin to recognise that always being influenced by other people means that you are being dictated to just as much as you used to be within your family. Being able to choose which ideas from outside and which of your own you would rather accept is an important part of growing up.

What else can friends offer?

Friendships are useful when you are feeling unsure and unsafe or lacking in confidence. Everyone feels more confident in a group. Some people get too confident. Just listen to a group of school-children shouting at each other on a bus, then look at how timid and shy they become when by themselves. There is safety in numbers and in feeling part of a crowd. But it is wise to watch that you do not get carried away in the excitement of a group and do things that you would never do alone or might regret later.

You are likely to form close friendships with one or two people, rather than a large group. Most friendships are two-way affairs—you give something to the relationship and you gain something from it.

You may find that you feel differently about yourself with different friends, or even with the same friend on different occasions. Sometimes you are a leader, sometimes you are led, sometimes you are a protector, sometimes protected. In the course of most friendships you learn as much about yourself as you learn about your friend.

Possibly the most difficult part of friendship is dealing with your emotions or your friend's emotions, when either of you is upset. Have you been able to express angry feelings with a good friend without destroying the friendship? If so, do you know what you did to make it easier for you and easier for them? If a friend does something you seriously disapprove of, can you still be their friend? You may have been faced with a situation where a person upset you so much either by their behaviour, or by letting you down, or by teasing you, that you decided that you could no longer be friends with them. Being able to apologise and admit you are wrong is never easy, but that is a necessary part of friendship, if it is to flourish. So also is being able to trust and be trusted, and accept and feel accepted by the other person.

Sometimes, learning to say 'no' can be an important part of friendship. Learning to regulate how close you get, or how dependent you become on a particular relationship, is difficult enough. Some friends become inseparable and spend all their time together, other friendships are maintained by occasional meetings only, spread over a long time. Maybe you have a cousin or someone you meet on holidays once a year, and feel just as friendly with them as someone you see every day.

The most important thing about friendships is that both of you feel you are gaining from the relationship and that you are not being taken advantage of or manipulated by this other person for their own gain. Friendship needs a careful balance between what you want and what your friend wants.

How do you choose your friends?

Usually you do not—it just happens! Some people like you, and you like some people, and sometimes the feeling is mutual. At school you are thrown together with people of the same age, studying similar subjects, playing similar games, and often from similar family backgrounds and similar neighbourhoods. But, once you leave school, making and keeping friends is less easy. Yet having relationships in adult life is just as important as having friends when you are growing up.

Making friends after school

You are more likely to make friends if you put yourself into situations where you will meet people—rather than just stay at home. For example, you could go on holidays, especially activity holidays (eg youth hostelling), or join a youth club or sports club; you could visit the local community centre, take an adult-education class, join a pen-pal club, or go hospital visiting.

Male and female friendships

Girls seem to make closer relationships than boys do, in their teenage years. They tend to confide and share their problems, share secrets about boyfriends or problems at

home, and they can often be supportive and caring towards each other. Sometimes they gossip! Often they are loyal to each other, but occasionally become competitive, for instance if they are after the same boy.

Boys are generally more wary of close relationships with each other. They may prefer groups of friends, and try to keep the conversation at a superficial level when personal problems are touched on. They may joke, or boast, or pretend, rather than reveal their true feelings. There is often more rivalry in boys' relationships with each other, and they may prefer to remain on safer topics such as work or hobbies, rather than talk about themselves and their problems. Boys are expected to be masculine, assertive, tough, not easily upset, insensitive, uncaring, big, strong, confident and self-sufficient.

But many are not like this. Girls meanwhile are expected to be feminine, attractive, in need of protection, uninterested in work and unambitious, and of course girls do not fit this stereotype either. A sensitive boy, or a tough girl, may feel they must pretend to be someone they are not; you should recognise that most boys have as many feminine characteristics as girls have masculine ones. The two sexes are much closer in their emotions and in the need for relationships than these sex-role stereotypes suggest. You should ignore them and be yourself.

Parents' disapproval of friends

Parents may feel a friend is unsuitable: they may think the friend is exploiting you, diverting you from work, inhibiting or overwhelming you. Their fears may be genuine and even justified, or they may be a cover for their own jealousy of your relationship with your friend, or their envy of the fun you are having, or the hurt they feel that you no longer need them as you did when younger. The important thing with parents is to try to understand what it is that concerns them, and to try to reassure them that you understand their fears and that you too recognise the pitfalls that they can see, but that you feel mature enough to handle both the challenge of this friendship and your own relationship with them.

Personal friendships after marriage

Married couples must decide how much time they are to spend with each other doing things and making friends as a couple, and how much they maintain their own personal relationships with individual friends. It can be very important, particularly for mothers stuck at home with small children, to have their own friends to share their experiences, problems and outings with during the day, perhaps even looking after each others' children on occasions. Similarly after marriage men may continue to enjoy the company of their friends for golf, football or even the occasional drink. It is important for married couples to find a balance between keeping their own personal friends and having joint friends within the marriage. Too much of one or the other makes the individual and the marriage more vulnerable.

People without friends

Some people choose to be solitary, others would like to have friends but cannot take that first step. Maybe you could make it for them. If you are a shy person, remember that most people like a listener, and if you can think of a few important questions to ask people about themselves, then you are well on the way to making friends. Waiting for them to take the first step is not a good idea. Try rehearsing in front of the mirror or pretending you are a confident person. Most of us role-play the sort of person we would like to be before we become that person in reality.

Sociopaths

These are people who do not have any regard for other people's feelings. They are self-centred and pre-occupied with their own needs. Beware of them, and even more, beware of becoming one of them. A good relationship is a balancing act between what you need and what your friend needs. Each should give and each should gain.

Brothers and sisters (siblings)

These are very special friendships. You cannot choose them—your link is a genetic one. Because you cannot avoid your relationship with your sisters and brothers, and because this family tie is such a long-term one, you often behave with a brother or sister the way you would never dream of behaving with friends outside the family. Some husbands and wives treat each other in this way too.

Do you have more rows with your siblings than you do with your friends, and insult and criticise them more? Do you rarely have a good word to say for them? Many siblings are like this, yet if anyone outside the family should criticise their brother or sister, or if a brother or sister becomes ill or is injured, they would be the first to be upset, and would prove the most loving, the most caring and the most loyal.

Amongst children, sibling rivalry (as we call it) is often just puppy play. You are trying out ways of coping with the aggression and rivalry you will encounter in the real world when you are older, and it is useful to have experienced it. But you may become locked into a more destructive pattern. If you find that you and your brothers and sisters need to compete for parental attention by frequently criticising each other, or putting each other down, or telling tales, you should each ask yourselves whether your parents really are being unfair to you in particular, or whether you are being thoughtless and immature. Have you considered the effects you may be having on each other? What about the effect you must be having on your parents, wearing them down with repeated arguments?

It is better to aim for a constructive withdrawal from each other, and avoid destructive rows. If you do not feel good about the relationships in your family, then try changing the way *you* behave—it is the only thing you can control.

5. Family Relationships

Have you noticed how your family relationships change with the passage of time?

You start as a child looked after by your parents.

Then you grow into a young adult (you are nearly there) and hope that your parents will treat you as one.

Then you become a parent yourself and 'parent' first your own children, and possibly later your own parents, as they become old and frail and child-like. And the cycle repeats itself, your own children eventually treating you as a child.

You are at that difficult stage, neither child nor adult. Your parents are more accustomed to having a relationship with you as a child and may have difficulty in accepting that you are growing up. Let us look at some of the things that influence your relationship with your family at this particular stage.

Where you come in the pecking order

Are you the eldest child, the youngest child, one in the middle, or an only child? Try to think of the advantages and disadvantages of being in your particular place in the family. Which position would you rather have? Some people think the eldest child has the hardest time, because they have to teach their parents how to be parents. Others think the youngest child, or the only child, has the hardest time, because their parents want to cling on to the last (or only one) in the nest and stop them growing up. The ones who are somewhere in the middle often complain of being unnoticed or left out.

The size of your family also affects your experience of growing up. If you think your parents have too many or too few children, have you decided how many children *you* would like to have? Do you think you would be able to make each one feel special and 'wanted', while they are growing up? It is hard to believe that it may only be a few years before you too are in your parents' position, so it is good to think about your own family-planning well ahead of time.

Your gender (which sex you are)

Parents tend to treat boys and girls differently, especially in the teenage years. But even in childhood, a son is encouraged to behave like a man and a daughter to be ladylike. This is called 'sex-role stereotyping'. It may cause problems for children of either sex, becaust most people are a complex mixture of so-called masculine and feminine behaviours and emotions. Boys need to cry and to be cuddled just as much as girls need to fight or shout.

Have you noticed that, in families where parents follow traditional roles, there is a lack of balance between male and female influence over the children? In most homes, the mother is much more involved in parenting than the father, and is likely to spend much more time with the children. This means that girls have the advantage of a same-sex model to copy, but they also have the disadvantage of a same-sex rival who is around a lot of the time. Boys have the advantage of their mother being the opposite sex (do mothers spoil boys more than girls?) but the disadvantage of having less contact with their same-sex model—their father.

You may have only one parent. This may be a good thing if the alternative is two unhappy parents, but it means that you will miss out on the influence of whichever parent is missing (not always the father). If you are from a single-parent family, you may have been able to find someone else to substitute for the missing parent-figure. It might be an uncle or aunt, a friend's Dad, or even one of your teachers.

Many parents seem to have 'double standards' with regard to the behaviour of sons and daughters. Sons are encouraged to explore the world and become experienced, experimenting with relationships and sowing their wild oats to get it out of their system before they settle down with their chosen wife. But parents feel more anxious about daughters. They fear that because they are not as physically strong as their sons, they are more prey to physical attack, especially at night, that they are more at risk of sexual misadventures (that may end in unwanted pregnancy), and that their reputation is more at risk if they stay out late, become experienced and street-wise. What do you think? How will you be with your own daughters and sons?

Why are the teenager years difficult for parents?

Your parents may have very mixed feelings about you growing up—glad you are nearly adult, yet sorry to see you move away from them. And you yourself may have confused feelings about growing up—feeling strong and independent one day, but needing your Mum or Dad to cheer you up the next.

Parenting is probably *the* most important task that people undertake in their lifetime, yet it is a subject that rarely gets taught, despite its complexity and importance. It is left to chance—people tend to 'hope for the best', or else they parent their own children in the way that they themselves were looked after.

Parents can often turn to books or magazines when they feel anxious about looking after a young baby, but once their children are teenagers, they will be less disposed to turn to the experts for help. After 16 years of being a parent, they probably think they have got it right, and they certainly will not want to admit to you that they are not sure what to do. But they may well be searching for reassurance, all the same. Maybe you can give them the odd compliment or two. There is little doubt that with the social changes that have come about in the last twenty years, they cannot rely on using the same parental approach as their parents did.

By the time you have reached your present age, most of their basic parenting will have been done. By now, you should know what your parents' attitudes and values are—what they think is right and wrong about different lifestyles and behaviours. You may reject much of what they think and have your own ideas, but it is surprising how many young people eventually end up with ideas and conclusions very similar to those of their own parents.

If you are lucky, your parents may have assumed that by now you can take some responsibility for looking after or 'parenting' yourself, and that they can replace some of their parental responsibility with a less restrictive kind of concern.

What you need to know about parenting

Parenting means surrounding a youngster with the three Cs—a *caring, controlled*, yet *challenging* environment that will encourage safe and healthy development. The ultimate aim is to produce happy, independent adults who can parent themselves, who can look after their own needs, yet be sensitive to the needs of others.

In time, you may be looking after not only yourself, but your own offspring too. So these hints may be doubly useful; but it is important to remember never to stop looking after yourself, even if you have children of your own.

When you were a tiny baby, you needed to feel completely loved and accepted, and perfectly safe and protected. Care and control were crucial. A tiny baby cannot be spoilt by giving it such security. It is much more likely to be 'spoilt' if it is allowed to feel anxious, unloved, unsafe or naughty. As a tiny child, you were too young to want many challenges, but you would have needed plenty of cuddling and talking to—and as you began to learn and understand more, you would have needed a more stimulating environment in which to develop. Your parents should have provided an expanding 'box' filled with love (care), praise (encouragement), and interesting things to do (challenges), and been prepared to listen to you as well as to teach. The box should also have had a clearly defined framework of limits and controls that were safe, appropriate and fair for your particular stage of development.

When you are young, your parents should decide on the boundaries and limits of your behaviour, not you. Youngsters who think *they* are in control, and can manipulate their parents, usually feel unsafe and frightened. Children need to know that someone else is in authority. They then quickly learn what is wrong, dangerous or naughty. Their parents' criticism, or the punishment they get (provided these are fair), act as alarm-signals, telling them that they have gone over the limits of what is acceptable. Most important of all, children learn best what is *right* by hearing praise and encouragement when they are being good. Unfortunately, parents tend not to notice when things are going well. When you are a parent yourself, remember to praise your children when they are behaving well, rather than simply nagging when they are misbehaving.

Parents and teenagers

Persuading parents that you are ready to care for yourself and control your own life is not easy; independence should be asked for a bit at a time, rather than all at once. Convincing them that you are capable is made more difficult if you behave like a child—sulking, slamming doors, rebelling if you do not get your own way. Parents feel an understandable reluctance and anxiety during the handover period. It may simply be that they have lived a lot longer than you, have experienced a lot more and understand better the pleasures, pains and pitfalls that lie ahead for you, sensing that you are not yet ready or able to make some decisions for yourself. Or it may be that you confuse them by seeming mature and self-confident one minute, and needing your family's support and advice the next.

No-one passes smoothly from childhood to adulthood overnight, and you and your family should be prepared for a pattern of behaviour in which you swing from one extreme to the other, and should not lose heart. You will never succeed in your own decision-making until you have had practice at it, gained experience, and learnt from your own mistakes. Your parents should give you the moral support and encouragement you need at this time, without too much interference or destructive criticism. You should in turn play fair with them, sticking to your word and building up their confidence that you can now take on this job for yourself.

Your parents may have other complex reasons for resisting your growing up—their fear of the empty home in a few years' time, their loss of role as parents and their increasing age; their envy of the new and greater opportunities that face you as a teenager, with cheap travel, exciting clothes and a greater choice of lifestyles than was available to them; their fear that you may remain unemployed and unable to leave home, an overgrown cuckoo in the nest; their jealousy about your relationships with other people; problems in their own marriage that may have been avoided while they were busy looking after you, which they fear may resurface once you have left. Most of these problems belong to your parents and not to you, but it is useful to recognise the possibility of their existence and reassure wherever possible. Learning to see your parents as real people with problems of their own is all part of growing up.

Common areas of concern and disagreement

Your ideas about caring for yourself and controlling yourself may be very different from your parents'.

Remember that your parents will inevitably remain concerned for you long after their control has faded. That is what human relationships and affection are all about. Remember too that as you gain responsibility for caring for yourself, so you acquire the responsibility of caring for your parents' feelings, of reassuring them and reducing their level of anxiety; this is all part of your new adult responsibility.

We should examine the more practical and physical areas of concern—matters that need careful negotiation between parents and young people if there is to be a smooth and gradual transfer of responsibility.

Money

What is a fair amount for you to receive if you are unwaged? How much should you give your parents once you have a job? Who dictates what you spend your money on, once it has been handed over? You should by now have already learnt some degree of responsibility about how you spend your money, and your parents will know that bailing you out each time you are in difficulties will not teach you to be financially responsible.

Clothes, hair and make-up

A sensible young person will understand and tolerate parents' concern or embarrassment about their experimentation with their appearance, perhaps reserving really freaky appearances for when their parents are away.

Lifestyle

The most difficult time is between the ages of 14 and 18. There are many areas of contention, such as alcohol, smoking, homework, housework and friends. Some of these are controlled outside your family by the laws of the land—no alcohol under 18, no sex under 16, no selling cigarettes to youngsters, statutory protection of under-16-year-olds who are in moral danger.

All these issues, and many more, are bound to be important in your home, unless you have a very exceptional family. The question is, have you determined who controls what, and, where appropriate, attempted to negotiate a handover of responsibility.

If you think you have taken over some of the responsibilities, have you informed your parents clearly, and have they agreed? And most important, have you been fair, and stuck to your word? The real problem in all this is that even when you have taken over all the decision-making yourself, you can never be as free as you would be if you lived alone. While you continue to live in a family, your behaviour and lifestyle inevitably have implications for others. But the important point about this stage in your life is that you begin to take over deciding what is right and fair, both for you and the family, and accept the responsibility for acknowledging that maybe you were wrong and should apologise and try doing better next time. This is the stage of give and take.

You must give way as much as other members of the household do, if you are going to coexist as adults together in your parents' house. Remember that once you are over 18, you are a new adult living in your parents' home. Territorial rights, responsibilities and privacy must be re-negotiated.

Privacy

Privacy is a precious commodity if you live in a small, busy household. But as you leave childhood, it becomes increasingly important. Both you and your parents need to have a territory that is your own, even if it is simply your bed and a chest of drawers. You need the freedom to organise your territory.

You need the privilege to be on your own at times and

the dignity of privacy for your bodily functions. You now need the right to chose how much physical contact you wish to have with your family and may find yourself withdrawing from close contact.

Occasionally parents, step-parents or other relatives get into an emotional confusion about what is appropriate behaviour between them and young people. Some may even force young people into having sexual experiences with them, threatening them with violence if they protest. If you know anyone trapped within such a problem; encourage them to share their difficulties with a *trusted* adult.

Sick parents

You may have physically or mentally ill parents, and may have had to look after them for some time, emotionally or practically. This can make it difficult for you to be young, to rebel, and to develop a lifestyle for yourself. Yet it is your right and privilege to grow up and establish a life for yourself. You may need to discuss these problems with a person outside your family. Some young people, faced with difficult or demanding parents, escape from home the moment they are 16, either by running away, getting pregnant, or getting married far too soon. They usually end up as unhappy and trapped in their new life as they were at home. Even if conditions are terrible at home, it is better for you to try and separate from your parents gradually, establishing new emotional and practical support systems rather than rushing into intimacy with one other person. If you have sick parents, it is possible to continue your relationship with them even if you are not living in the same house.

Single parents

A single-parent family can go through considerable strain during the teenage years, as one parent has to shoulder all the anxieties about the growing children.

If you are the child of a single parent, make sure you reassure them that you have your own best interests at heart as much as they have. They may have organised their life in a particular way, so that it centres on you, if their relationship with you is their main one; this will make it harder for you to grow up and leave home.

You may become a single parent yourself. There are undoubted difficulties in shouldering the parenting role alone for 18 years—though single parents often make extremely good parents if they have a lot of friends with whom to share the joys and pains. Nevertheless, you should think very carefully before you decide to get pregnant if you are alone. *Never* let it happen by accident.

Divorced parents

You may have a mother here and a father there, or vice versa. In your teenage years you might find the balance of your relationship with them changing slightly as you find one or other parent more sympathetic to your needs. It is always difficult to remain on good terms with both parents when you are living with one, but it is in your best interest to try and persevere, even if they seem to have very different views about what is appropriate for you. It should become easier once you are adult. Take the best you can from each of them and give the best you can in return. You will have learnt a lot of useful things about relationships from their experiences, which may help you to make fewer mistakes yourself.

Working mothers

Over half of mothers now work, either part-time or full-time. If a mother does have a job, this need cause the children no problems as they grow up, provided they receive adequate care and love. Indeed, many studies suggest that part-time working Mums are more cheerful than full-time housewives. But mothers themselves may feel guilty if they are not at home all day, catering for their children. Others feel guilty if they are at home without a job.

Undoubtedly, women's roles and expectations have changed dramatically over the last 30 years. You should examine your own views on this subject, whether you are male or female, because this may affect your choice of work and training (some jobs are easier to do part-time) and your choice of partner when you marry. Some women and men now share the child-rearing, each believing that they have the right to parent, and the right to a job of their own with an income. It is a good idea to have thought these things out, before you get married.

Unusual fathers

In the past, parents were thought of as having very separate roles and characteristics:

—Dad: financial provider, disciplinarian, strict, remote, rarely seen, insensitive and ambitious;

—Mum: loving, domestic, available, easily manipulated, sensitive, concerned about others.

Nowadays such role distinctions are more blurred. But if you have a father who is absent a lot because of his work (perhaps he is a sailor, salesman, or oil-rig worker), or is away for another reason (perhaps he is in prison), the family can have a problem in shifting from one-parent power to two-parent power when he returns. It can be especially difficult during the teenage years. Or your father may be a step-father and not your real Dad. That can be a real problem too. Each of you competes for your mother's affection; he is not sure what role he should take on where you are concerned, and you resent him assuming that he should, and can, behave like a real Dad. Have you been able to discuss this with your Mum or even with him?

It sometimes helps, once you are older, to discuss family problems with an outsider, your guidance teacher, your family doctor or a youth counsellor, especially if you feel trapped in a difficult situation. Talking about difficulties not only helps to get them into a clearer perspective, it sometimes produces new ways of coping with old problems.

6. Your relationship with Yourself

This is perhaps the most important chapter of the book, because your relationship with yourself is your most important relationship. Wherever you are, whoever you are with, whatever you are doing, you are always there watching and making judgements about yourself. And what *you* think about yourself should be just as important as what other people think about you. Some people get this balance wrong. Either they are too heavily influenced by other people's views and have little regard for their own, or they are the opposite—they take no notice of what other people think.

What is a normal person?

Everybody's personality is different, but there are certain patterns of behaviour and certain characteristics that can be grouped together to give a picture of the average, well-balanced, mature adult person—the person you are aiming to be.

Would you agree that such a person should be:
—independent and self-sufficient (doesn't need Mum any more)
—adaptable and flexible (can adjust to different situations)

- capable of friendship (even though self-sufficient)
- able to fill time effectively (in work or hobbies)
- able to control emotions (avoiding extremes)
- sensitive to other people's needs (as well as their own)
- comfortable with sexuality (although not necessarily having a relationship with anyone).

But very few people are completely normal. You probably have quite a lot of quirks, like anybody else, but, as you grow older, the sort of person you are will evolve and mature. Think back to the way you were five years ago. It was probably very different from the way you are today, and five years from now you will be different again.

Personality variations

Here is a list of some personality variations that can cause difficulties; they are common in teenagers. Some of the labels might have applied to you at some point. But if, as an adult, you become trapped with an extreme version of one of these variations, things could become difficult for you and your family relationships.

A person may be:
- dependent or immature (always leaning on someone or something)
- obsessional and rigid (likes routine and tidiness; and is upset by change or challenge)
- schizoid or withdrawn (avoids making friends)
- paranoid or oversensitive (prickly like a hedgehog and always ready to take offence)
- hysterical or theatrical (poor control of emotions, swinging from too happy to too sad—a common teenage problem)
- neurotic (constantly feeling anxious or depressed)
- sociopathic or extremely selfish (having no regard for other people's feelings).

You will see that many of these descriptions are the opposite of those in the list for the well-balanced normal adult.

Sometimes people are grouped in a different way, as *extroverts*—people who enjoy company and are usually the life and soul of the party, and *introverts*—people who prefer their own thoughts and company.

But whatever your basic personality type, you still have a considerable degree of choice about, and influence over, the way you think, the way you feel, and the way you behave. Therefore, you cannot simply blame your personality for your behaviour, because you are the person responsible for regulating it.

Your inner self

Your inner self is the being that silently talks to you and watches what you are doing.

Your relationship with this inner you is your most important relationship. This inner person is a sort of replacement for your own parents. When you were younger, your real parents helped you to decide how to think, how to feel and how to behave; now this inner parent has to weigh up the pros and cons, make judgements, and help you to decide for yourself.

Your thoughts, feelings and behaviour are powerfully linked together and each of these three affects the others.

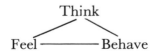

The way you think

Are you more critical of yourself than you are of other people? Most people look at others through rose-tinted spectacles, but look at themselves through black ones. They see the good points in other people and the bad points in themselves. But when you really think about it, that's a daft way round. It means you are constantly having negative (destructive) thoughts about yourself, which undermine your self-confidence, your feelings, your ability to cope, and your behaviour. You should try to think *encouraging* thoughts about yourself from now on.

A golden rule is, always try to talk to yourself as you would talk to a good friend—that is with encouragement and reassurance, and not with criticism and contempt.

The way you feel

Being your own Mum and Dad where your emotions are concerned can be more difficult. Up to now you may have relied on your parents cheering you up or calming you down, but it is extremely important to learn to deal with your emotions by yourself. Common feelings that cause special problems include anger, anxiety, depression and excitement. The following suggestions may help you to handle emotional storms by yourself:

— Recognise when you are feeling upset or uptight; often people refuse to acknowledge emotions because they are too painful to admit.
— Identify what emotion it is your are experiencing. It might be anger, excitement, depression, anxiety or guilt, and there are many others.
— Ask yourself why you are feeling that way.

If you are really upset, you may need to share your feelings with another person to help clear your mind, so that you can think straight. Discovering why you are feeling so upset can be more difficult than you would think. If there is no-one around to discuss your feelings with, writing them down can sometimes help you to get your thoughts straight and may help you to put your finger on the underlying reason for your emotions. Until you have discovered why you are feeling the way you are, it is quite difficult to decide how to deal with your emotions. One thing is certain, if you do not find constructive ways of handling painful emotions, they can get out of hand and destroy your well-being. Feeling too excited, too angry or too depressed can be dangerous not only to your health, but to your friendships as well.

If possible, try to calm yourself down a bit (thump a cushion or have a secret weep) before you try to discuss it with the person that made you upset. Sometimes it is easier to look for alternative ways that *you* could think or behave to stop you feeling upset, rather than expecting someone else to change for your sake.

People who are feeling depressed often find that if

they do something constructive—for example, go for a walk, write a letter, play with a child, visit their Granny, or go to the pictures, they start to feel more cheerful because of what they are doing.

Behaviour

How you choose to behave is partly governed by your basic personality, but is much more influenced by how you are feeling at the moment. If you are feeling cheerful, what you decide to do will be very different from what you would decide to do if you were feeling depressed. But, because of the links, what you decide to do can also influence your emotions. If you are doing something you rate okay, useful or interesting, it makes you *feel good*; if you are doing something that you despise, it makes you *feel bad*.

Once you are an adult, you are totally responsible for your own behaviour, unless you are seriously mentally ill or in prison.

We have already looked at some aspects of your behaviour in relationships with other people in the earlier chapters. But now we should consider your behaviour towards yourself.

Your outer self

Your outer self is the person you reveal to the outside world. When you meet a new person, your reactions to them will be based on the way they look, the way they carry themselves (their style) and, of course, the way they behave towards you. Other people will judge you in exactly the same way.

Your appearance

During the teenage years, you are liable to exaggerate the importance of your appearance and even become preoccupied by it, forgetting that how you carry yourself and how you behave are probably more important. You are saddled with your own particular body and, like everyone else, you are probably dissatisfied with it. But even if it is not what you would have chosen, it is the best you have, so look after it. You may already have discovered that your relationship with your body can have quite an impact on your life. Try to experiment and find out what makes your body and you live harmoniously together.

How you can influence your body

What you wear
Clothes usually have more effect on the wearer than on the observer, so your choice of clothing is important in your relationship with yourself. If you choose to wear a low-cut blouse, tight jeans, black leather, or school uniform, you feel different, and other people react differently. You must experiment to find out what reactions in yourself and in other people you feel comfortable with. Getting new clothes can often help to make you feel less depressed, for example.

Your hair
Whatever your gender, how you feel can have a profound effect on your hair, and your hair can have a profound effect on how you feel. Again, you will need to experiment with your hair to find a style that suits your mood and produces a desirable reaction in other people. If you choose a really way-out style, do not be surprised if you receive a way-out response from other people.

Your style

If you were asked to play the part of an old man, a delinquent 16-year-old, a sexy young thing, a caveman, or a shy person, you'd know how to do it. Most people have the techniques for play-acting, but cannot decide which role in the play they want to have. Only by trial and error can you discover which way of walking into a room, which way of chatting someone up, which way of sitting by yourself and walking down the street is going to feel right for you. Sometimes self-confidence comes after you have played the part of being a self-confident person for a while. Most people are shy and unsure of themselves underneath, but gradually acquire confidence as they become more experienced and more successful. Remember that how you present yourself to the outside world affects how you feel, as well as how other people feel about you. Even if you are feeling depressed or anxious, it is possible to act a part, saving those secret feelings for those you trust and can confide in.

Fitness

Servicing the body that carries you around is important. Keeping fit should not simply be for health freaks and sporting types; you will feel better if you exercise your body regularly. Try it and see.

Food

If you eat too much, you feel bloated and look fat. Some people use this fat to hide behind. If you eat too little, you look too thin, and you may be using this tight control over your appetite and weight as a weapon to make you feel successful and to make your family feel anxious about you. If trying to keep your weight low has become the main focus of your life, ask yourself whether there are other more constructive and useful ways of making yourself feel a success and of getting your family's attention and interest.

Drink and smoking
These have been put together because they are both potentially dangerous habits. Once you are over 18, you will be able to choose how much you drink, and will learn that alcohol has both pleasures and pains. A regular heavy drinker is a poor companion, a disastrous husband or wife, and is endangering their own health. Although women can, and often do, drink as much as men, their bodies cannot handle alcohol so well, and they are more at risk of liver failure. If a man drinks over 35 units of alcohol a week (1 unit is half a pint of beer, a single measure of spirits or a glass of wine), he is at risk of becoming an alcoholic. If a woman drinks more than 21 units a week, she too is at risk. Remember that most alcoholic drinks contain a minimum of 75 calories per drink.

Smoking is a killer. If you smoke, ask yourself why you do. Usually you start smoking and drinking to create the right impression, to look grown up, to hide your embarrassment and shyness, and give you Dutch courage. Some people think they have more style with a cigarette or a glass in their hand. Then they get hooked on the nicotine or alcohol, and a habit that started off as a walking stick to give them confidence ends up as a crutch they cannot do without and the crutch finally turns into a coffin. People who smoke regularly die younger, from cancer, from heart disease and from chest complaints.

Drugs
Hard drugs, soft drugs, glue-sniffing and tranquillisers —all these offer artificial and sometimes dangerous and illegal ways of altering your mood. When you are high on drugs, you kid yourself that life is great. But once the trip is over, real life looks even greyer. Using drugs is a self-destructive way of coping—it drags you and your mates down and destroys all hope. You should look for

real and constructive ways of making yourself feel great, not rely on artificial ways.

General health
Some people become extraordinarily preoccupied about their health. They are labelled hypochondriacs and are constantly worried about their bowels, their catarrh, earwax, the state of their throats, backache, etc., etc. If you are worried about your health, discuss it with a trusted doctor or nurse. If you have no confidence in their judgements, seek a second opinion. If you never believe what you are told, you might be using your concern about your body to stop you facing the real problems of getting on with your life and sorting out your relationships with other people.

Remember that some people (and you might be one of them) do have chronic health problems, such as diabetes or asthma, or perhaps a physical handicap or disability that permanently influences their life. But even with illness, you are still a normal person, with normal feelings and normal relationships. So do not let illnesses, or your body, or your appearance, get in the way of your relationship with yourself and your relationship with other people.

7. Sexual Relationships

A loving relationship is a private and personal thing. If you feel romantically involved with another person, your friendship often involves some physical expression of your feelings.

Sometimes your sexual urges may seem to be out of all proportion with the emotional involvement you have with a particular person. Because of this, when making personal decisions about who you want to go out with, and how far you want to go with them physically, it may be a help to have certain facts at your disposal.

This chapter offers you some of these facts and tells you where you can get more advice if you need further information or help. You may be lucky enough to be able to discuss your personal life and its problems with your parents, or you may have an older relative or friend in whom you can confide; many families find this subject almost impossible to talk about.

Help! I've no special relationship

Although your body has gone through puberty, you do not automatically feel ready to get involved with the opposite sex (or in some cases the same sex). By 19, half of all teenagers will have had had some sexual experience and half will not, so, whether you have a close relationship or not, you are normal.

Some people choose to learn to live by themselves before experimenting with that special relationship. Others feel they are missing out if they do not have a boyfriend or girlfriend available all the time. Ask yourself what makes *you* feel more mature, having a personal relationship because you feel you must have one, or choosing to have one when a person you like comes along. Individual circumstances (for example, living in an isolated place) obviously affect your ability to make such a choice. Some successful people have chosen to stay single all their lives—and live very happily. It's your decision!

Can you cope with your adult body?

By 18 most people have gone through puberty. If your body has not changed by that age (that is, if you have not sprouted pubic hair, and developed breasts or a deeper voice), then you should seek medical advice.

Girls have to learn to cope with periods (some use tampons in preference to traditional sanitary towels, for greater freedom), and to accept that once they start to menstruate, if they go 'too far' physically, they are likely to get pregnant. They also have to learn to cope with boys whistling at them and paying more attention to them (or worrying if they don't) and deciding what sort of young woman they want to appear to be, in the eyes of other people, e.g. sexy, sporty, studious, shy, etc.

Boys have to learn to cope with the unexpected erections (sometimes these come at embarrassing times) and with the occasional wet dream, which is a natural emission of semen usually occurring at night. They also have to cope with girls taking more interest in them and feeling self-conscious about their shape and size and how they look.

Your personality plays a far more important part in your relationship with other people than your physical appearance, so do keep it in perspective. Remember that a few spots or pimples or slightly larger breasts, which may be agony to their owner, are hardly noticed by an observer. What sort of a person you *are* is far more important than how you look.

Can you cope with your adult body's new responses and new ideas?

Most young men discover for themselves that erections can happen not only by chance but by choice. Some young women also discover that in addition to becoming fertile, their body is beginning to show sexual responses (increased secretion from the vagina and a feeling of warmth and fullness in the pelvic region), and these too can be produced by choice. Stimulating your own body (masturbation) is not in itself harmful, but worrying about it or becoming preoccupied with it can be. Keep this in perspective too.

Many young people have sexual fantasies in their teens. These may take the form of all sorts of odd or even kinky ideas and day-dreams. It is as though their minds are rehearsing all sorts of exciting sexual possibilities. As with most day-dreams, reality may be very different from the fantasy. Therefore, do not worry if your fantasy-life seems really way out. When you start becoming involved with a real person, common sense or embarrassment will soon bring you back to earth. Sorting out fact from fantasy (think of those TV ads for chocolate or shampoo) takes time and experience. Some people say that girls tend to fantasise about romance whereas boys fantasise about sex. Is that true for you?

Who should I go out with?

We all want to love and be loved—but by whom?

A daft question—only *you* can make that sort of decision, although your parents may express some strong views about your choice. Some people find themselves preferring to stay with a group of friends rather than pair off. That is no problem. In fact, the earlier you try to settle down into a permanent relationship, the more likely it is to go wrong later on. Only you can choose who feels right for you, and at the beginning you rarely have a clue who that might be. It is a good idea to experiment with a few loosely attached friendships, till you begin to learn who you are and what you want from a relationship. Only then can you work out what you want to give to a relationship and who deserves to get if from you.

Some people find themselves feeling closer to friends of the same sex and cannot be bothered with the problems of boyfriends or girlfriends. They may even find themselves wanting to get emotionally or even physically close to them. A few (4% of boys, 1% of girls) will go on as adults to enjoy same-sex (gay) relationships. That is their choice, and others should respect it as their own private decision, just as your choice of partner is a private one too. Homosexuals do not harm society, but the same cannot be said in reverse.

Why do we have the urge to pair off?

Babies are the product of a sexual relationship between man and woman. Babies flourish best in an environment maintained by Mum and Dad, although many nowadays are of necessity brought up in one-parent families.

But our urge to pair off starts long before we feel ready to have a baby. Think of the many different reasons why young people choose to go out with each other:

—strong physical attraction
—close friendship which gradually develops into romance
—need for affection and special attention
—need to prove to yourself or to your mates that you can get a boy or girl friend
—companionship

and lots more.

Usually there are several reasons why you go out with someone, and their reasons may be very different from yours, so watch out! You may have thought they loved you as much as you love them, when in fact they were just using you for their own purposes. It is always wise to protect yourself a bit until you really know and can trust another person. That takes time and experience, so slow down before becoming emotionally involved or committed to them.

What about physical contact?

If you like someone, you want to be close to them and cuddle and kiss them. You may even feel like this with small babies, with your parents and some of your friends. But in a special relationship, sexual feelings are added to those natural demonstrations of friendship. Be careful. You can have sexual feelings towards people you do not feel particularly attracted to, and these are dangerous, because they may lead you to get attached to someone you do not really like as a person. Casual sex is not only a bad thing emotionally; you are also much more likely to catch venereal disease or get pregnant. A few youngsters find themselves sexually involved or sexually exploited by older people or even relatives, and this can be emotionally damaging. It is your right to seek advice if this happens to you. It is *not* your fault—it is theirs.

How far you decide to let your physical expression of affection go is also your personal decision, once you are over 16. Before then, it is illegal to have sex; even if the boy is under 16 too, he can be prosecuted for unlawful sexual activity.

However close you feel to your partner, it is important not to feel pressurised into going further sexually than you wish. Similarly, you should not be forcing other people to go too far. The further you go sexually, the more likely you are to get into deep water—physically and emotionally.

Remember that if genital organs get close together too soon, you may not have the skills or maturity to handle the consequences. It is a highly dangerous situation. It is far safer to stick to cuddling and caressing and fondling each other. Only after appropriate contraceptive precautions have been taken, and the emotional commitment fully considered, should you ever contemplate full intercourse. In some religions, there are strong rules about pre-marital sex (sex before marriage) and many of you will want to follow the teachings of these religions.

Some useful facts about sex

—A single unprotected act of intercourse can cause pregnancy.
—You can get pregnant if you make love standing up—even if you do not enjoy it and even if you have a bath afterwards.
—It is possible to enjoy the full range of sexual responses without having intercourse.
—If a boy really loves a girl, he will want to protect her from the risks of emotional hurt and pregnancy. She should want to protect him from these too.
—Whether you are having regular or irregular sex, you need protection against pregnancy.

Why do parents worry so much about sex?

From their own experiences (and they must have experienced it to have had you) they are aware that sex is a powerful urge that can lead to a lot of pleasure, but can also cause a lot of pain. Usually they are trying to protect you against the pain rather than help you to discover the pleasures! Common anxieties centre on their fear of an unwanted pregnancy, of you becoming promiscuous (having a lot of casual sexual encounters), or getting venereal disease, or being raped. They also worry that you might get emotionally or physically hurt, or settle down too soon, concentrating on a single relationship at the expense of everything else in your life—exams, work, sport, hobbies, friends. They may feel jealous and resentful of your involvement with this other person. They may be wanting to protect themselves from embarrassment at your behaviour, or from the realisation that you are growing up quickly, and that they are losing their role as parents.

If you are fond of your parents, you will want to reassure them that you too are aware of the pitfalls and dangers they see in sex, but that you are now old enough and responsible enough to protect yourself from these. Being sensitive to their anxieties is a good way to convince them of your maturity and encourage them to hand over the decision-making to you. If you are lucky, you will be able to share some of your anxieties about your sexual development with them too. But do not expect them to give an unbiased opinion; they are bound to be more concerned about your welfare than anything else.

Where to go for further advice

If you are sure that neither your parents nor a close relative can listen to your problems (have you really tried to talk to them?), then you should try some of the other sources of help that may be available to you. Remember, help will not come to you—you must make the first move. You could get help from:

- the guidance staff at school
- youth workers in youth clubs or community centres
- the minister or priest at the local church
- marriage guidance counsellors (e.g. The National Marriage Guidance Council or Catholic Marriage Advisory Council), who will see single as well as married people

—your family doctor (general practitioner), who should treat your enquiries with confidence
—the family-planning clinic, which may have a young person's clinic.
—Brook Advisory Centre, which will advise you on sexual relations, contraception and unwanted pregnancy
—Pregnancy Advisory Service, which gives advice on the termination of pregnancy.
—special hospital clinics for sexually transmitted diseases.

Settling down

When you are young, you fall in and out of love frequently. Looking back, you realise that on most occasions you were just infatuated, but *thought* you were in love.

Deciding with whom you want to spend the rest of your life is a huge decision, and should never be taken without a great deal of thought. If you have experienced a few close relationships beforehand, they might have helped you to sort out what kind of person you feel relaxed with.

Remember that the powerful emotion of being in love might cloud your judgement. Liking and trusting a person, and feeling that you could be friends for a long time, are just as important as being in love with them—so take your time. Most people feel more comfortable with someone from their own background and culture, with similar expectations about what being a husband or wife will mean.

Remember that most of the romantic views about marriage are sheer fantasy. Marriage will not make you into a different sort of person. Nor will it improve or alter your lover in any predictable way. Marriage does not work miracles—it merely acts as an extra bond and commitment between you, makes a public statement about your relationship, and provides a securer base for raising a family.

Some important ingredients for a successful marriage are:

- —being able to *tell* each other what you like and do not like (good communications)
- —being able to *listen* to your partner's views sympathetically
- —being able to *compromise*—to give and take
- —being able to *share* decision-making and responsibility
- —being able to *trust* each other and respect each other's feelings
- —being able to express anger without being destructive.

Before you get married, it is as well to have discussed your attitudes and expectations about life after marriage.

In particular—how do you both feel about having children, about extra-marital relationships, about working wives, about financial responsibilities, about who makes decisions, about time for hobbies, about keeping personal friends, and about the role your respective parens will play in your lives after you are married? Topics such as these can so often become major problems in the lives of married couples—such difficulties may have affected your parents' marriage too. So be warned and think things through carefully beforehand.

The majority of people *do* marry and the majority of marriages *do* survive and result in children just like you.

So the whole cycle repeats itself—with you, as an adult, not only enjoying and worrying about your own personal relationships, but feeling concern about your children's personal relationships too.

Good luck with *your* life's cycle and those personal relationships.

Town of Markham Public Libraries
Unionville Branch
15 Library Lane
Unionville, Ontario L3R 5C4